JUICES and
SMOOTHIES

Publications International, Ltd.

CONTENTS

RAISE A GLASS TO YOUR HEALTH

If your idea of a drink in the morning is a glass of OJ next to your breakfast plate, you're in for a delicious, nutritious surprise. You can enjoy juices and smoothies from a cornucopia of colorful, flavorful fruits and vegetables using an electric juicer or blender and the simple recipes and tips in this book. As you'll quickly discover, these beverages are an easy and convenient way to fit more green, nutrient-rich fruits and veggies into your daily diet. And that's a proven path to better health and a lower risk of disease.

WHY START DRINKING YOUR PRODUCE?

We've all heard the news—from doctors, nutritionists, the media and even the U.S. government: We need to eat more fruits and vegetables. These gifts from the garden (and orchard) are naturally rich sources of many vitamins and minerals that are essential to life. But more than that, research has shown time and again that getting plenty of fruits and vegetables can help us function at our best and protect us from a host of health problems, including heart disease and certain cancers. Scientists suspect these benefits come from the unique combination of nutrients—including vitamins, minerals and special plant chemicals called phytonutrients—that are certainly present in produce.

With so much to gain, it just makes good sense to give green fruits and vegetables a major place in our daily meals. Indeed, many experts say we should aim to fill half of our plate with fruits and vegetables at every meal. And the greater the variety of produce we choose, the more likely we are to cover our nutritional bases and gain the widest protection against everyday illnesses and chronic diseases.

Sadly, most of us don't come close to getting the minimum 2 cups of fruits and 2½ cups of vegetables a day that are recommended in the government's latest Dietary Guidelines for Americans. If you're one of those people—if you struggle to get the amount or variety of produce that your body deserves on a daily basis—these drinks can help bridge the gap. They are also a great way to give yourself some additional, natural "health insurance."

Making juices and smoothies makes exploring new produce options very simple. Preparing most fruits and vegetables often involves little more than washing the produce and feeding it into your machine. In the process of trying recipes, you'll come across plenty of fruits and vegetables that you'll want to start adding to your plate as well as to your juicer or blender.

TIPS FOR BETTER JUICES/SMOOTHIES

The following tips can help you improve your experience:

- Use the freshest fruits and vegetables available to obtain the best tasting and most nutritious juice.

- Make only as much juice as you need right away. With no preservatives, fresh juice begins to lose flavor and nutrients immediately after juicing.

- For best results, select produce that is ripe (or if necessary, nearly ripe) and still on the firm side.

- Wash your hands with soap and warm water immediately prior to working with produce or any other food.

- Always wash fruits and vegetables thoroughly—even those you intend to peel—before juicing them. Otherwise, debris and bacteria from the surface can be transferred to the fresh fruit within when you cut into or handle it. Use a vegetable brush or other clean, firm-bristled brush, if necessary, to remove embedded debris.

- Wash and, if necessary, cut, peel or otherwise prepare produce just before putting it into the juicer or blender.

- Cut out any bruised, soft or damaged areas from produce before putting it into the juicer or blender.

- If you're using produce that has a hard, waxy or inedible skin or rind, peel it before using.

- Large or hard pits, stones or seeds should be removed from produce before it is fed into the machine.

- If the flavor of the juice or smoothie is too intense, try adding more mildly flavored fruits or vegetables or those with a higher water content (celery or cucumber, for example) to the mix the next time you make it. Doing so should help dilute the overpowering taste.

- Once you've made at least some of the recipes in this book, try doing some experimenting to create your own personalized juice and smoothie combinations. After all, variety is the spice of life!

Note: *For the recipes in this book, 1 serving is 6 to 8 ounces. Keep in mind that the tremendous variation in ingredients (large or small apples or carrots, juicy or not-so-juicy citrus fruit, etc.) as well as the type of juicer or blender you use may give you different results.*

LEAN AND GREEN

EASY BEING GREEN

2 cups watercress
2 parsnips
2 stalks celery
½ cucumber
4 sprigs fresh basil

Juice watercress, parsnips, celery, cucumber and basil. Stir.

Makes 2 servings

THE ENERGIZER

2 tomatoes
½ cucumber
8 green beans
½ lemon, peeled
Dash hot pepper sauce

Juice tomatoes, cucumber, green beans and lemon. Stir in hot pepper sauce until well blended.

Makes 2 servings

EASY BEING GREEN

CITRUS SPROUT

1 cup brussels sprouts
4 leaves romaine
   lettuce
1 orange, peeled
½ green apple
½ lemon, peeled

Juice brussels sprouts, romaine, orange, apple and lemon. Stir.

Makes 2 servings

BEDTIME COCKTAIL

½ head romaine
   lettuce
2 stalks celery
½ cucumber

Juice romaine, celery and cucumber. Stir.

Makes 2 servings

CITRUS SPROUT

GREEN QUEEN

1 cup fresh spinach
1 cup fresh cilantro
2 stalks celery
5 leaves kale
½ cucumber
½ green apple
½ lemon, peeled
½ inch fresh ginger, peeled

Juice spinach, cilantro, celery, kale, cucumber, apple, lemon and ginger. Stir.

Makes 2 servings

KALE-APPLE-CARROT

3 carrots
2 stalks celery
1 green apple
3 leaves kale
½ cup fresh parsley

Juice carrots, celery, apple, kale and parsley. Stir.

Makes 2 servings

GREEN QUEEN

MEAN AND GREEN

1 green apple
2 stalks celery
3 leaves kale
½ cucumber
½ lemon, peeled
1 inch fresh ginger, peeled

Juice apple, celery, kale, cucumber, lemon and ginger. Stir.

Makes 2 servings

TONGUE TWISTER

2 green apples
1½ cups arugula
½ cup fresh cilantro
½ jalapeño pepper
1 cup coconut water

Juice apples, arugula, cilantro and jalapeño pepper. Stir in coconut water until well blended.

Makes 2 servings

MEAN AND GREEN

VEGGIE DELIGHT

1 carrot
1 stalk celery
1 beet
1 green apple
½ small sweet onion

Juice carrot, celery, beet, apple and onion. Stir.

Makes 2 servings

MINT JULEP JUICE

1 green apple
1 cup fresh spinach
1 cup fresh mint
1 stalk celery

Juice apple, spinach, mint and celery. Stir.

Makes 1 serving

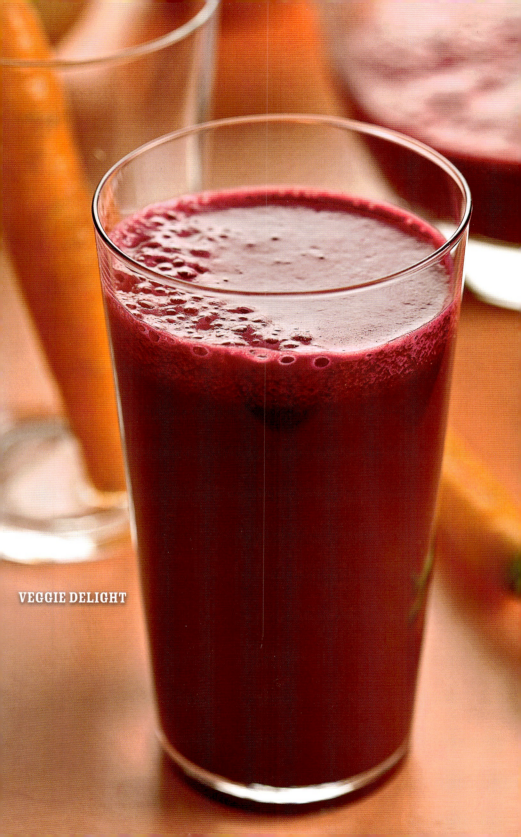

VEGGIE DELIGHT

HEADACHE BUSTER

1 cup cauliflower florets
1 cup broccoli florets
1 green apple

Juice cauliflower, broccoli and apple. Stir.

Makes 1 serving

HEART HEALTHY JUICE

2 tomatoes
1 cup broccoli florets
1 cucumber
1 carrot
1 stalk celery
½ lemon, peeled
1 clove garlic

Juice tomatoes, broccoli, cucumber, carrot, celery, lemon and garlic. Stir.

Makes 2 servings

HEADACHE BUSTER

FIERY CUCUMBER BEET JUICE

1 cucumber
1 beet
1 lemon, peeled
1 inch fresh ginger, peeled
½ jalapeño pepper

Juice cucumber, beet, lemon, ginger and jalapeño pepper. Stir.

_____

Makes 2 servings

SUPER BETA-CAROTENE

4 carrots
1 green apple
4 leaves bok choy
2 leaves kale
½ inch fresh ginger, peeled

Juice carrots, apple, bok choy, kale and ginger. Stir.

_____

Makes 2 servings

FIERY CUCUMBER BEET JUICE

APPLE CARROT ZINGER

4 carrots
2 green apples
¼ cucumber
1 inch fresh ginger, peeled

Juice carrots, apples, cucumber and ginger. Stir.

Makes 2 servings

PEACH SURPRISE

1½ cups fresh spinach
1 peach
3 sprigs fresh mint

Juice spinach, peach and mint. Stir.

Makes 1 serving

APPLE CARROT ZINGER

FENNEL CABBAGE JUICE

1 green apple
¼ small green cabbage
½ bulb fennel
1 lemon, peeled

Juice apple, cabbage, fennel and lemon. Stir.

Makes 2 servings

ARTHRITIS TONIC

4 spears asparagus
3 carrots
3 stalks celery
1 green apple
1 cup broccoli florets
1 cup fresh parsley

Juice asparagus, carrots, celery, apple, broccoli and parsley. Stir.

Makes 2 servings

FENNEL CABBAGE JUICE

AMAZING GREEN JUICE

1 cucumber
1 green apple
2 stalks celery
½ bulb fennel
3 leaves kale

Juice cucumber, apple, celery, fennel and kale. Stir.

Makes 2 servings

UP AND AT 'EM

2 cups fresh spinach
1 green apple
1 carrot
1 stalk celery
¼ lemon, peeled
1 inch fresh ginger, peeled

Juice spinach, apple, carrot, celery, lemon and ginger. Stir.

Makes 2 servings

AMAZING GREEN JUICE

GREEN ENERGY

2 stalks celery
2 green apples
6 leaves kale
½ cup fresh spinach
½ cucumber
¼ bulb fennel
½ lemon, peeled
1 inch fresh ginger,
    peeled

Juice celery, apples, kale, spinach, cucumber, fennel, lemon and ginger. Stir.

Makes 4 servings

PEARS & GREENS

3 pears
2 cups fresh spinach
5 leaves kale
1 cucumber
1 cup sugar snap peas
½ lemon, peeled

Juice pears, spinach, kale, cucumber, sugar snap peas and lemon. Stir.

Makes 3 servings

GREEN ENERGY

WALDORF JUICE

2 green apples
6 leaves beet greens,
    Swiss chard or
    kale
2 stalks celery

Juice apples, beet greens and celery. Stir.

Makes 2 servings

TANGY TOMATO BASIL

2 tomatoes
1 cup fresh spinach
4 sprigs fresh basil
½ lemon, peeled

Juice tomatoes, spinach, basil and lemon. Stir.

Makes 2 servings

WALDORF JUICE

CLEANSING GREEN JUICE

4	leaves bok choy
1	stalk celery
½	cucumber
¼	bulb fennel
½	lemon, peeled

Juice bok choy, celery, cucumber, fennel and lemon. Stir.

Makes 2 servings

JICAMA FRUIT COMBO

1½	cups strawberries
1	cup cut-up peeled jicama
1	green apple
½	cucumber
2	sprigs fresh mint

Juice strawberries, jicama, apple, cucumber and mint. Stir.

Makes 2 servings

CUCUMBER BASIL COOLER

1 cucumber
1 green apple
½ cup fresh basil
½ lime, peeled

Juice cucumber, apple, basil and lime. Stir.

Makes 2 servings

SHARP APPLE COOLER

3 green apples
1 cucumber
¼ cup fresh mint
1 inch fresh ginger, peeled

Juice apples, cucumber, mint and ginger. Stir.

Makes 2 servings

CUCUMBER BASIL COOLER

GREEN JUICE

- 2 cups fresh spinach
- 2 cucumbers
- 1 pear
- ½ lemon, peeled
- 1 inch fresh ginger, peeled

Juice spinach, cucumbers, pear, lemon and ginger. Stir.

Makes 2 servings

TRIPLE GREEN

- ½ honeydew melon, rind removed
- 1 cucumber
- 4 leaves kale

Juice honeydew, cucumber and kale. Stir.

Makes 2 servings

GREEN JUICE

JUICER'S PARADISE

MOJO MOJITO JUICE

1	cucumber
1	pear
1	cup fresh mint
½	lime, peeled

Juice cucumber, pear, mint and lime. Stir.

Makes 2 servings

PEAR RASPBERRY

2	pears
1½	cups raspberries
½	cucumber

Juice pears, raspberries and cucumber. Stir.

Makes 2 servings

MOJO MOJITO JUICE

SUNSET BERRY

1 cup strawberries
1 orange, peeled
½ lime, peeled

Juice strawberries, orange and lime. Stir.

Makes 2 servings

SWEET VEGGIE JUICE

1 cup fresh spinach
1 carrot
½ cucumber
1 plum
½ cup strawberries
¼ cup cherries, pitted

Juice spinach, carrot, cucumber, plum, strawberries and cherries. Stir.

Makes 2 servings

SUNSET BERRY

PINEAPPLE-MANGO-CUCUMBER

¼ **pineapple, peeled**
1 **mango, peeled and pitted**
1 **cucumber**
½ **lemon, peeled**

Juice pineapple, mango, cucumber and lemon. Stir.

Makes 3 servings

RAINBOW JUICE

8 **leaves Swiss chard**
1 **pear**
1 **green apple**
1 **beet**
1 **carrot**
¼ **head green cabbage**

Juice chard, pear, apple, beet, carrot and cabbage. Stir.

Makes 2 servings

PINEAPPLE-MANGO-CUCUMBER

TROPICAL VEGGIE JUICE

5 leaves kale
⅛ pineapple, peeled
½ cucumber
½ cup coconut water

Juice kale, pineapple and cucumber. Stir in coconut water until well blended.

Makes 2 servings

APPLE MELON JUICE

¼ honeydew melon, rind removed
¼ cantaloupe, rind removed
1 green apple
3 leaves kale
3 leaves Swiss chard

Juice honeydew, cantaloupe, apple, kale and chard. Stir.

Makes 2 servings

TROPICAL VEGGIE JUICE

COOL PEAR MELON

¼ **honeydew melon, rind removed**

1 **pear**

½ **cucumber**

Juice honeydew, pear and cucumber. Stir.

_____

Makes 3 servings

INVIGORATING GREENS & CITRUS

2 **oranges, peeled**

1 **grapefruit, peeled**

1 **zucchini**

½ **cup broccoli florets**

½ **inch fresh ginger, peeled**

Juice oranges, grapefruit, zucchini, broccoli and ginger. Stir.

_____

Makes 2 servings

COOL PEAR MELON

CRANBERRY APPLE TWIST

2 green apples
¾ cup cranberries
½ cucumber
½ lemon, peeled
1 inch fresh ginger, peeled

Juice apples, cranberries, cucumber, lemon and ginger. Stir.

Makes 3 servings

REFRESHING STRAWBERRY JUICE

2 cups strawberries
1 cucumber
¼ lemon, peeled

Juice strawberries, cucumber and lemon. Stir.

Makes 2 servings

CRANBERRY APPLE TWIST

ORANGE FENNEL SPROUT

2 oranges, peeled
2 stalks celery
1 bulb fennel
1 cup alfalfa sprouts

Juice oranges, celery, fennel and alfalfa sprouts. Stir.

Makes 2 servings

DRINK A RAINBOW

2 carrots
¼ pineapple, peeled
1 green apple
1 pear
½ beet
¼ cup brussels sprouts
¼ cup broccoli florets

Juice carrots, pineapple, apple, pear, beet, brussels sprouts and broccoli. Stir.

Makes 3 servings

ORANGE FENNEL SPROUT

SWEET & GREEN

1 cup broccoli florets
¼ pineapple, peeled
2 stalks celery

Juice broccoli, pineapple and celery. Stir.

Makes 2 servings

VITAMIN BLAST

¼ cantaloupe, rind removed
1 orange, peeled
¼ papaya
2 leaves Swiss chard

Juice cantaloupe, orange, papaya and chard. Stir.

Makes 2 servings

SWEET & GREEN

JOINT COMFORT JUICE

2 cups fresh spinach
¼ pineapple, peeled
1 pear
1 cup fresh parsley
½ grapefruit, peeled

Juice spinach, pineapple, pear, parsley and grapefruit. Stir.

Makes 2 servings

PEAR GINGER COCKTAIL

1 pear
½ cucumber
½ lemon, peeled
1 inch fresh ginger, peeled
Ice cubes

Juice pear, cucumber, lemon and ginger. Stir. Serve over ice.

Makes 1 serving

POMEGRANATE-LIME-COCONUT JUICE

1 pomegranate,
  peeled
½ cucumber
1 lime, peeled
¼ cup coconut water

Juice pomegranate seeds, cucumber and lime. Stir in coconut water until well blended.

Makes 2 servings

SPICY APPLE PEACH

2 green apples
8 leaves mustard
  greens
2 stalks celery
1 kiwi, peeled
1 peach

Juice apples, mustard greens, celery, kiwi and peach. Stir.

Makes 2 servings

POMEGRANATE-LIME-COCONUT JUICE

SWEET CELERY

3 stalks celery
1 green apple
1 lemon, peeled
¼ cup raspberries

Juice celery, apple, lemon and raspberries. Stir.

Makes 2 servings

WORKOUT WARMUP

2 green apples
2 kiwis, peeled
½ cup strawberries
4 leaves kale
½ lime, peeled

Juice apples, kiwis, strawberries, kale and lime. Stir.

Makes 2 servings

SWEET CELERY

DOUBLE GREEN PINEAPPLE

4 leaves Swiss chard
4 leaves kale
¼ pineapple, peeled

Juice chard, kale and pineapple. Stir.

Makes 1 serving

POPEYE'S FAVORITE JUICE

2 cups fresh spinach
¼ pineapple, peeled
1 cup raspberries

Juice spinach, pineapple and raspberries. Stir.

Makes 1 serving

DOUBLE GREEN PINEAPPLE

MELON RASPBERRY MEDLEY

⅛ **honeydew melon, rind remmoved**

⅛ **seedless watermelon, rind removed**

⅓ **cup raspberries**

Ice cubes

Juice honeydew, watermelon and raspberries. Stir. Serve over ice.

Makes 2 servings

SWEET GREEN MACHINE

¼ **honeydew melon, rind removed**

2 **kiwis, peeled**

½ **cup green seedless grapes**

Juice honeydew, kiwis and grapes. Stir.

Makes 2 servings

MELON REFRESHER

¼ **cantaloupe, rind
   removed**
1 **pear**
1 **lime, peeled**
2 **sprigs fresh mint**

Juice cantaloupe, pear, lime and
mint. Stir.

Makes 2 servings

GREEN BERRY BOOSTER

1 **cup blueberries**
1 **cucumber**
1 **green apple**
4 **leaves collard
   greens, Swiss
   chard or kale**
½ **lemon, peeled**

Juice blueberries, cucumber, apple,
collard greens and lemon. Stir.

Makes 2 servings

MELON REFRESHER

KIWI TWIST

2 kiwis, peeled
2 pears
½ lemon, peeled

Juice kiwis, pears and lemon. Stir.

Makes 2 servings

KALE MELON

4 leaves kale
2 green apples
⅛ seedless watermelon, rind removed
¼ lemon, peeled

Juice kale, apples, watermelon and lemon. Stir.

Makes 2 servings

KIWI TWIST

CRANBERRY PEAR BLAST

2 **pears**
½ **cucumber**
¾ **cup cranberries**
¼ **lemon, peeled**
½ **inch fresh ginger, peeled**

Juice pears, cucumber, cranberries, lemon and ginger. Stir.

Makes 2 servings

GRAPEFRUIT REFRESHER

1 **grapefruit, peeled**
1 **green apple**
½ **cucumber**
¼ **beet**
2 **leaves Swiss chard**

Juice grapefruit, apple, cucumber, beet and chard. Stir.

Makes 2 servings

CRANBERRY PEAR BLAST

BRIGHT 'N' BLENDED

LEMON MELON CRÈME SMOOTHIE

3 cups cubed honeydew melon

½ (12-ounce) can thawed frozen lemonade concentrate

2 tablespoons vanilla low-fat yogurt

1 Combine honeydew, lemonade concentrate and yogurt in blender; blend until smooth.

2 Pour into three glasses.

_____

Makes 3 servings

LEMON MELON
CRÈME SMOOTHIE

HONEYDEW GINGER SMOOTHIE

1½ cups cubed
    honeydew melon

½ cup banana slices

½ cup vanilla nonfat
    yogurt

½ cup ice cubes

¼ teaspoon grated
    fresh ginger

1 Combine honeydew, banana, yogurt, ice and ginger in blender; blend until smooth.

2 Pour into three glasses.

_____

Makes 3 servings

TIP: Fresh fruit makes an excellent garnish for smoothies. Slice a small slit in any leftover fruit and hook it to the lip of the glass.

HONEYDEW GINGER
SMOOTHIE

LEMON BASIL SMOOTHIE

2 cups lemon sorbet

1 cup ice cubes

1 cup milk

1 container (6 ounces) vanilla yogurt

⅓ cup fresh lemon juice

2 tablespoons chopped fresh basil

2 teaspoons grated fresh lemon peel

1 Combine sorbet, ice, milk, yogurt, lemon juice, basil and lemon peel in blender; blend until smooth.

2 Pour into three glasses.

Makes 3 servings

TIP: Purée fresh basil leaves with a small amount of water and pour into ice cube trays. Store the frozen cubes in plastic freezer bags and use as needed.

MANGO-LIME COOLER

2 mangoes, peeled and cubed

2 cups cold water

1 cup ice cubes

½ cup sugar

½ cup fresh lime juice

1 Combine mangoes, water, ice, sugar and lime juice in blender; blend until smooth.

2 Pour into four glasses.

Makes 4 servings

LEMON BASIL SMOOTHIE

GOING GREEN

2 cups ice cubes

1 cup green seedless grapes

¼ honeydew melon, peeled and cubed

4 kiwis, peeled and quartered

2 tablespoons honey

1 Combine ice, grapes, honeydew, kiwis and honey in blender; blend until smooth.

2 Pour into four glasses.

___

Makes 4 servings

NOTE: Honeydew melon is an excellent source of vitamin C, which is essential for the formation and repair of collagen, a primary component of blood vessels and a type of tissue that holds the body's cells and tissues together. Vitamin C also promotes the normal development of bones and teeth.

GOING GREEN

TROPICAL GREEN SHAKE

1 cup ice cubes
1 cup packed
      stemmed kale
1 cup frozen tropical
      fruit mix*
½ cup orange juice
2 tablespoons honey
      or agave nectar

*Tropical fruit mix typically
contains pineapple, mango and
strawberries along with other fruit.

1 Combine ice, kale, tropical fruit mix, orange juice and honey in blender; blend until smooth.

2 Pour into two glasses.

Makes 2 servings

NOTE: Kale stands a head above other greens as an excellent source of beta-carotene and vitamin C, two antioxidants believed to be major players in the body's battle against cancer, heart disease, and age-related declines in vision and cognitive function. Kale is packed with readily absorbed calcium, a mineral that is vital to warding off the bone-thinning disease osteoporosis and may also help keep blood pressure in a healthy range.

TROPICAL GREEN SHAKE

GREEN ISLANDER SMOOTHIE

1 cup ice cubes

½ banana

¾ cup fresh pineapple chunks

½ cup packed torn spinach

½ cup packed stemmed kale

Combine ice, banana, pineapple, spinach and kale in blender; blend until smooth.

Makes 1 serving

NOTE: Bananas are not only beneficial to your health, they are a great ingredient that will add sweetness and creaminess to your smoothies.

GREEN ISLANDER
SMOOTHIE

KIWI PINEAPPLE CREAM

1 cup frozen
     pineapple
     chunks
1 container
     (6 ounces) key
     lime yogurt
1 kiwi, peeled and
     quartered
½ cup unsweetened
     coconut milk
1 tablespoon
     honey

1 Combine pineapple, yogurt, kiwi, coconut milk and honey in blender; blend until smooth.

2 Pour into two glasses.

Makes 2 servings

KIWI CHAI SMOOTHIE: Add ¼ teaspoon vanilla, ⅛ teaspoon ground cardamom, ⅛ teaspoon ground cinnamon, ⅛ teaspoon ground ginger and a pinch of ground cloves to the blender before blending.

SMOOTH MANGO SHAKE

2 very ripe mangoes,*
     peeled and cubed
1½ cups milk
1 cup vanilla ice cream
     or frozen yogurt
1 tablespoon fresh lime
     juice
¼ teaspoon ground mace

*Very ripe mangoes are essential for the flavor of this shake.

1 Combine mangoes and milk in blender; blend until smooth. Add ice cream, lime juice and mace; blend until smooth.

2 Pour into four glasses.

Makes 4 servings

KIWI PINEAPPLE CREAM

FROZEN FIZZ

- 2 **cups (16 ounces) ginger ale, divided**
- 1 **cup frozen unsweetened strawberries**
- 2 **tablespoons sugar**
- 2 **tablespoons fresh lime juice**

1 Combine 1½ cups ginger ale, strawberries, sugar and lime juice in blender; blend until smooth.

2 Pour into four glasses. Top with remaining ½ cup ginger ale.

Makes 4 servings

TROPICAL BREAKFAST SMOOTHIE

- 1 **can (20 ounces) pineapple chunks in juice, undrained**
- 1 **banana**
- 1 **cucumber, peeled and seeded**
- ½ **cup ice cubes**
- ½ **cup orange juice**
- ¼ **cup flaked coconut**
- 1 **tablespoon fresh lime juice**

1 Combine pineapple, banana, cucumber, ice, orange juice, coconut and lime juice in blender; blend until smooth.

2 Pour into four glasses.

Makes 4 servings

FROZEN FIZZ

BLUEBERRY AND BANANA FROZEN YOGURT SMOOTHIE

1½ cups fresh or frozen blueberries

1 banana

1 cup milk

¼ avocado, peeled and pitted

1 cup vanilla frozen yogurt

1 Combine blueberries, banana, milk and avocado in blender; blend until smooth. Add frozen yogurt; blend until smooth.

2 Pour into three glasses.

Makes 3 servings

KIWI STRAWBERRY SMOOTHIE

2 kiwis, peeled and quartered

1 cup frozen unsweetened strawberries

1 container (6 ounces) strawberry yogurt

½ cup milk

2 tablespoons honey

1 Combine kiwis, strawberries, yogurt, milk and honey in blender; blend until smooth.

2 Pour into two glasses.

Makes 2 servings

BLUEBERRY AND BANANA
FROZEN YOGURT SMOOTHIE

TROPICAL SMOOTHIE

2 mangoes,* peeled
   and cubed
   (about 1⅓ cups)

6 tablespoons fresh
   lime juice

3 tablespoons milk

3 tablespoons
   pineapple-
   orange juice

⅔ cup vanilla ice
   cream

*You can substitute 1⅓ cups
frozen mango pieces for the fresh
mango. Partially thaw the mango
before using it (microwave on
defrost for 1 to 2 minutes).

1 Combine mangoes, lime juice, milk
and pineapple-orange juice in blender;
blend until smooth. Add ice cream;
blend until smooth.

2 Pour into two glasses.

Makes 2 servings

BLACKBERRY LIME SMOOTHIE

1 cup frozen
   blackberries

1 cup milk

½ cup packed torn
   spinach

1 tablespoon sugar

1 tablespoon fresh
   lime juice

Combine blackberries, milk, spinach,
sugar and lime juice in blender; blend
until smooth.

Makes 1 serving

TROPICAL SMOOTHIE

BERRY FROST

1½ cups ice cubes
1 cup brewed green
   tea, at room
   temperature
1 cup water
½ cup frozen
   blueberries
1 tablespoon fresh
   lime juice
1 tablespoon honey
½ teaspoon grated
   fresh lime peel

1 Combine ice, tea, water, blueberries, lime juice, honey and lime peel in blender; blend until smooth.

2 Pour into two glasses.

Makes 2 servings

POM POM PLEASER

1 cup pomegranate
   seeds, divided
1 cup ice cubes
½ cup canned jellied
   cranberry sauce
½ cucumber, peeled
   and seeded
2 tablespoons
   pomegranate
   concentrate or
   syrup
2 tablespoons honey
3 sprigs fresh mint

1 Place 1 tablespoon pomegranate seeds in each of two serving glasses.

2 Place remaining pomegranate seeds, ice, cranberry sauce, cucumber, pomegranate concentrate, honey and mint in blender; blend until smooth.

3 Pour into prepared glasses.

Makes 2 servings

BERRY FROST

THE DAILY GREEN

GO GREEN SMOOTHIE

1½ cups ice cubes

1 cup packed torn spinach

½ cup vanilla almond milk

¼ cup vanilla low-fat yogurt

¼ avocado, peeled and pitted

1 teaspoon fresh lemon juice

1 teaspoon honey

Combine ice, spinach, almond milk, yogurt, avocado, lemon juice and honey in blender; blend until smooth.

Makes 1 serving

GO GREEN
SMOOTHIE

BLUE KALE SMOOTHIE

1½ cups ice cubes

1 banana

1 cup packed stemmed kale

½ cup fresh or frozen blueberries

¼ cup vanilla low-fat yogurt

1 Combine ice, banana, kale, blueberries and yogurt in blender; blend until smooth.

2 Pour into two glasses.

Makes 2 servings

POWERFUL POMEGRANATE SMOOTHIE

1½ cups blueberry-pomegranate juice

1½ cups strawberry sorbet

1½ cups fresh strawberries, sliced

1½ cups ice cubes

2 containers (about 4 ounces each) fresh blueberries

1 cup packed torn spinach

1 Combine blueberry-pomegranate juice, sorbet, strawberries, ice, blueberries and spinach in blender; blend until smooth.

2 Pour into five glasses.

Makes 5 servings

BLUE KALE
SMOOTHIE

ANTI-STRESS SMOOTHIE

2 **cups frozen blueberries**

1 **cup milk**

1 **cup vanilla frozen yogurt**

½ **avocado, peeled and pitted**

½ **cup ice cubes**

1 **tablespoon honey**

2 **sprigs fresh lavender**

1 Combine blueberries, milk, frozen yogurt, avocado, ice, honey and lavender in blender; blend until smooth.

2 Pour into four glasses.

Makes 4 servings

TIP: Add a garnish of fresh herbs to enhance and bring out certain flavors of your smoothie.

ANTI-STRESS SMOOTHIE

START-THE-DAY SMOOTHIE

1 package (16 ounces) frozen peaches, partially thawed

2 containers (6 ounces each) vanilla yogurt

¾ cup white grape juice

½ avocado, peeled and pitted

½ teaspoon vanilla

1 Combine peaches, yogurt, grape juice, avocado and vanilla in blender; blend until smooth.

2 Pour into three glasses.

Makes 3 servings

TIP: To thin out smoothies and add an extra boost of flavor, add 2 to 3 tablespoons of fruit juice to the blender.

START-THE-DAY
SMOOTHIE

SUPER SMOOTHIE

1 cup packed
   stemmed kale

1 cup packed baby
   spinach

1 cup ice cubes

1 banana

½ cup apple juice

1 Combine kale, spinach, ice, banana and apple juice in blender; blend until smooth.

2 Pour into two glasses.

Makes 2 servings

PEACHY BANANA SHAKE

1 cup packed torn
   spinach

1 cup milk

1 banana

½ cup vanilla ice cream

1 peach, peeled, pitted
   and sliced

1 teaspoon vanilla

1 Combine spinach, milk, banana, ice cream, peach and vanilla in blender; blend until smooth.

2 Pour into two glasses.

Makes 2 servings

PEAR-AVOCADO SMOOTHIE

1½ cups ice cubes

1 pear, peeled and cubed

1 cup apple juice

½ avocado, peeled and pitted

½ cup fresh mint leaves

2 tablespoons fresh lime juice

1 Combine ice, pear, apple juice, avocado, mint and lime juice in blender; blend until smooth.

2 Pour into two glasses.

Makes 2 servings

RISE 'N' SHINE SHAKE

1 cup milk

1 cup fresh strawberries, sliced

1 kiwi, peeled and quartered

¼ cup vanilla or strawberry frozen yogurt

1 to 2 tablespoons sugar

1 Combine milk, strawberries, kiwi, frozen yogurt and sugar in blender; blend until smooth.

2 Pour into two glasses.

Makes 2 servings

PEAR-AVOCADO SMOOTHIE

CREAMY STRAWBERRY-BANANA SHAKE

1½ cups ice cubes
½ banana
½ cup fresh strawberries, sliced
½ cup orange juice
¼ avocado, peeled and pitted

1 Combine ice, banana, strawberries, orange juice and avocado in blender; blend until smooth.

2 Pour into two glasses.

Makes 2 servings

REFRESH SMOOTHIE

1 cup ice cubes
½ cucumber, peeled and seeded
1 cup frozen mixed berries
4 teaspoons sugar
Grated peel and juice of 1 lime

1 Combine ice, cucumber, berries, sugar, lime peel and lime juice in blender; blend until smooth.

2 Pour into two glasses.

Makes 2 servings

CREAMY STRAWBERRY-BANANA SHAKE

SALAD BAR SMOOTHIE

1½ cups ice cubes

½ banana

½ cup fresh raspberries

½ cup fresh strawberries, sliced

½ cup fresh blueberries

½ cup packed torn spinach

Combine ice, banana, raspberries, strawberries, blueberries and spinach in blender; blend until smooth.

Makes 1 serving

NOTE: Fresh or frozen berries can be used interchangeably in most smoothie recipes. When using frozen fruit, reduce the amount of ice used.

SALAD BAR
SMOOTHIE

PEACHES AND GREEN

1 cup ice cubes
1 cup packed torn spinach
1 cup frozen peaches
¾ cup vanilla almond milk
2 teaspoons honey

1 Combine ice, spinach, peaches, almond milk and honey in blender; blend until smooth.

2 Pour into two glasses.

Makes 2 servings

NOTE: Spinach contains an amazingly rich mix of essential nutrients with antioxidant functions, including vitamins C, E, A and the minerals manganese, selenium and zinc. If you don't eat enough greens every day, try drinking them instead!

PEACHES
AND GREEN

SPA SMOOTHIE

1 cup ice cubes

½ cucumber, peeled and seeded

½ cup cubed cantaloupe

½ cup fresh strawberries, sliced

¼ cup plain nonfat Greek yogurt

1 tablespoon sugar

1 teaspoon grated fresh lemon peel

1 Combine ice, cucumber, cantaloupe, strawberries, yogurt, sugar and lemon peel in blender; blend until smooth.

2 Pour into two glasses.

Makes 2 servings

TIP: Adjust the thickness of your smoothie by varying the amount of ice used. Less ice will result in a thicker smoothie.

SPA SMOOTHIE

SWEET GREEN SIPPERS

HONEYDEW AGUA FRESCA

¼ **honeydew melon, rind removed and cubed**

¼ **cup fresh mint leaves**

¼ **cup fresh lime juice**

2 **tablespoons sugar**

1½ **cups club soda, chilled**

4 **lime wedges**

4 **mint sprigs**

1 Combine honeydew, mint, lime juice and sugar in blender; blend until smooth. (Mixture may be blended in advance and chilled for several hours.)

2 Pour into 4-cup measuring cup and stir in enough club soda to measure 4 cups.

3 Pour into four glasses. Garnish with lime wedges and mint sprigs. Serve immediately.

Makes 4 servings

HONEYDEW
AGUA FRESCA

LEMON-LIME ICEE

4 cups ice cubes

2 cans (12 ounces each) frozen limeade concentrate

1 cup sparkling water

Juice of 1 lemon

Lemon and lime slices

1 Crush ice in blender. Add limeade concentrate, sparkling water and lemon juice; blend until smooth.

2 Pour into two glasses; garnish with lemon and lime slices.

Makes 2 servings

LIME JUICE SPARKLERS

2 cups pineapple juice

2 cups lemon-lime soda

1 cup fresh lime juice

¼ cup grenadine

1 lime, cut into wedges

¼ cup sugar

Ice cubes

1 Mix pineapple juice, soda, lime juice and grenadine in small pitcher.

2 Rub lime wedge around rims of five glasses. Pour sugar into deep bowl; dip rims of glasses in sugar. Fill glasses to just beneath rim with ice cubes. Pour juice mixture over ice. Garnish with lime wedges.

Makes 5 servings

LEMON-LIME
ICEE

MANGO-LIME VIRGIN MARGARITA

- 2 **lime wedges**
- 2 **tablespoons coarse salt**
- 1 **mango, peeled and cubed**
- 1 **cup ice**
- ½ **cup fresh lime juice**
- ⅓ **cup water**
- ¼ **cup sugar**
- 3 **tablespoons orange juice**
  Additional lime slices

1 Rub rims of two margarita glasses with lime wedges; dip in salt.

2 Combine mango, ice, lime juice, water, sugar and orange juice in blender; blend until smooth. Pour mixture into prepared glasses. Garnish with lime slices.

Makes 2 servings

LIMEADE

- 4 **cups cold water, divided**
- ⅔ **cup sugar**
- 1 **cup fresh lime juice**
- 1 **cup ice cubes**
  Lime slices

1 Combine ⅔ cup water and sugar in small saucepan. Cook and stir over medium heat until sugar is dissolved. Cool completely.

2 Combine lime juice, remaining water and sugar syrup in large pitcher. Stir until blended. Serve over ice. Garnish with lime slices.

Makes 6 servings

VARIATION: This recipe can also be adapted for fresh lemonade. Use about 6 lemons to make 1 cup lemon juice.

MANGO-LIME VIRGIN MARGARITA

STRAWBERRY-BASIL SPARKLERS

Basil Simple syrup
(recipe follows)

4 cups fresh
strawberries,
sliced

Ice cubes

Club soda

1 Prepare Basil Simple Syrup.

2 Combine strawberries and Basil Simple Syrup in blender; blend until smooth.

3 Fill eight glasses with ice. Divide strawberry mixture among glasses; fill with club soda.

Makes 8 servings

BASIL SIMPLE SYRUP

1 cup fresh basil
leaves

⅔ cup sugar

⅔ cup water

Combine all ingredients in small saucepan; cook and stir over medium heat until sugar is dissolved. Remove from heat; cool completely. Pour through fine-mesh sieve; discard basil. Store in refrigerator up to 1 week.

Makes ⅔ cup

STRAWBERRY-BASIL SPARKLERS

LIME-APPLE-GREEN TEA SPRITZER

¼ cup plus 1 tablespoon sugar, divided
4 cups brewed green tea
¼ cup fresh lime juice
2 cups apple juice
2 cups seltzer water
1½ cups ice cubes
6 slices green apple

1 Stir 1 tablespoon sugar into brewed tea; chill.

2 Combine remaining ¼ cup sugar and lime juice until sugar is dissolved. Add apple juice, seltzer and lime juice mixture to tea.

3 Divide ice among six glasses. Pour spritzer over ice. Float 1 apple slice in each glass.

Makes 6 servings

LIME-APPLE-GREEN TEA SPRITZER

GRAPEFRUIT-MINT ICED WHITE TEA

- 2 teaspoons chopped fresh mint
- 4 cups brewed white tea
- 1 cup fresh grapefruit juice
- ½ cup sugar
- 1 cup ice cubes

1 Stir mint into brewed tea; cool 10 minutes. Mix grapefruit juice and sugar until sugar is dissolved; add to tea.

2 Divide ice among four glasses. Pour tea over ice.

Makes 4 servings

TIP: If plain white tea is unavailable, use a tropical-flavor tea for best results.

CRANBERRY-LIME PARTY PUNCH

- 7½ cups cranberry juice cocktail
- ½ cup fresh lime juice
- ¼ cup sugar
- 2 cups ice cubes
- 1 cup ginger ale or lemon-lime soda
- 1 lime, sliced

1 Combine cranberry juice, lime juice and sugar in punch bowl; stir until sugar dissolves.

2 Stir in ice, ginger ale and lime slices. Pour into ten glasses.

Makes 10 servings

GRAPEFRUIT-MINT ICED WHITE TEA

MINT-GREEN TEA COOLERS

2 **bags green tea**

4 **thin slices fresh ginger (about 1 inch each)**

7 **or 8 large fresh mint leaves, roughly torn**

2 **cups boiling water**

2 **cups crushed ice**

1 Place tea bags, ginger and mint leaves in teapot or 2-cup heatproof measuring cup. Add boiling water; steep 4 minutes. Remove tea bags, ginger and mint leaves; discard. Cool tea to room temperature.

2 Pour 1 cup crushed ice into each of two tall glasses. Divide tea between glasses.

Makes 2 servings

TIP: Squeeze a lime wedge into each cooler before serving.

MINT-GREEN
TEA COOLERS

METRIC CONVERSION CHART

VOLUME MEASUREMENTS (dry)

1/8 teaspoon = 0.5 mL
1/4 teaspoon = 1 mL
1/2 teaspoon = 2 mL
3/4 teaspoon = 4 mL
1 teaspoon = 5 mL
1 tablespoon = 15 mL
2 tablespoons = 30 mL
1/4 cup = 60 mL
1/3 cup = 75 mL
1/2 cup = 125 mL
2/3 cup = 150 mL
3/4 cup = 175 mL
1 cup = 250 mL
2 cups = 1 pint = 500 mL
3 cups = 750 mL
4 cups = 1 quart = 1 L

VOLUME MEASUREMENTS (fluid)

1 fluid ounce (2 tablespoons) = 30 mL
4 fluid ounces (1/2 cup) = 125 mL
8 fluid ounces (1 cup) = 250 mL
12 fluid ounces (1 1/2 cups) = 375 mL
16 fluid ounces (2 cups) = 500 mL

WEIGHTS (mass)

1/2 ounce = 15 g
1 ounce = 30 g
3 ounces = 90 g
4 ounces = 120 g
8 ounces = 225 g
10 ounces = 285 g
12 ounces = 360 g
16 ounces = 1 pound = 450 g

DIMENSIONS

1/16 inch = 2 mm
1/8 inch = 3 mm
1/4 inch = 6 mm
1/2 inch = 1.5 cm
3/4 inch = 2 cm
1 inch = 2.5 cm

OVEN TEMPERATURES

250°F = 120°C
275°F = 140°C
300°F = 150°C
325°F = 160°C
350°F = 180°C
375°F = 190°C
400°F = 200°C
425°F = 220°C
450°F = 230°C

BAKING PAN SIZES

Utensil	Size in Inches/Quarts	Metric Volume	Size in Centimeters
Baking or Cake Pan (square or rectangular)	8×8×2	2 L	20×20×5
	9×9×2	2.5 L	23×23×5
	12×8×2	3 L	30×20×5
	13×9×2	3.5 L	33×23×5
Loaf Pan	8×4×3	1.5 L	20×10×7
	9×5×3	2 L	23×13×7
Round Layer Cake Pan	8×1½	1.2 L	20×4
	9×1½	1.5 L	23×4
Pie Plate	8×1¼	750 mL	20×3
	9×1¼	1 L	23×3
Baking Dish or Casserole	1 quart	1 L	—
	1½ quarts	1.5 L	—
	2 quarts	2 L	—